NATURE UNFOLDS

MOUNTAINS AND DESERTS

GERARD CHESHIRE

Illustrated by

PETER BARRETT

CRABTREE
www.crabtreebooks.com

MOUNTAINS AND DESERTS

DESERTS

CONTENTS

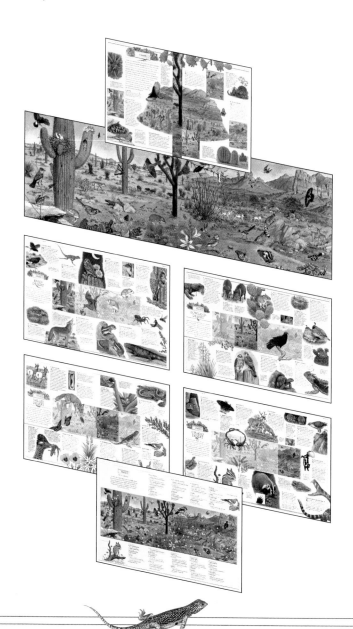

MOUNTAINS

CONTENTS

Deserts

The American south-western desert is an area of land that receives little rainfall over a long period of time. Few plants are able to grow in the dry soil. Plants that can survive in the desert, such as cactus plants and Joshua trees, compete for what little moisture is available. Animal life in the desert is made up of **species** that have **adapted** to dry, or **arid** conditions. Many animals get the water they need from eating plants. Unlike desert animals, plants cannot move out of the heat, so they grow in places where shadows fall. Plants keep cool by allowing water to **evaporate** from their leaves and stems. Plants also need to take in water to survive, so they have ways of storing as much water as possible. Water is important in the desert, because life cannot exist without it.

▼ The landscape of south-west American deserts includes areas of cactus plants (foreground), **eroded** rocks (right mid-ground), dried-up **watercourses** (center), and rocky hills (background). Rain is rare, but some animals and plants have adapted to take advantage of the occasional **flash floods**.

▲ PLANTS AS PROTECTION
A roadrunner makes its nest in the middle of a cactus bush. Many desert animals use the sharp spines of cacti as protection from **predators**.

SCAVENGERS ➤
Carcasses rot very quickly in the desert heat. **Scavengers** such as the vulture (right) can eat rotten meat without getting ill.

◀ DESERT BASIN
Low areas of desert are often the hottest regions. The air is so still that it **insulates** the ground like a blanket. In these places, animals and plants need to be well adapted to survive the harsh conditions. Most animals avoid the daytime heat by hiding under rocks or **burrowing** underground. Burrows are underground tunnels that are cooler than the surface.

◀ KEEPING COOL
Reptiles such as snakes and lizards are well suited to desert conditions because they rely on the heat of the sun for energy. In addition, snakes keep cool under rocks, and lizards keep their body off the hot ground.

LOWLAND DESERT ➤
Most people think of deserts as endless seas of shifting sand stretching to the horizon, but most deserts do not contain very much loose sand. In the lowlands of American south-western deserts, the ground is often very hard, and baked dry by the heat of the sun. Animals and plants here are sparse and scattered, because it is hard work for animals to burrow and difficult for plants to take root.

DESERT VALLEY ➤

E ven in the driest regions there are ways for plants and animals to find enough water to survive. Rain does occasionally fall, and **water vapor** in **humid** air forms into dew during the night. In the valley of the south-western desert, water from higher ground sometimes travels underground and reappears near the surface in springs.

DESERT FLOWERS ➤

After rainfall, flowering plants appear in a desert. To ensure **pollination,** they bloom at the same time flying insects hatch. The plants also need to produce seeds while there is enough water in the ground.

▼ UPLAND DESERT

A t higher levels, deserts are often cool and windy. Areas of higher **altitudes** are fairly dry, so it is still difficult for animals and plants to survive. The terrain is shaped by the erosion of rocks and soil by flash floods. These areas are described as semi-desert because of the patches of tough, leafy plants that grow there.

CACTUS PLANTS ➤

Cacti are plants especially adapted for life in the arid climate and poor soils of southern North American deserts. Many species of cacti have fluted, or ribbed, stems so that they can expand or contract depending on the amount of water available to them during the year.

◄ HARRIS' HAWK

Harris' hawks are similar to other hawks in appearance. Unlike other **birds of prey**, Harris' hawks hunt in groups, using teamwork to locate and capture **prey**. This means each hawk gets more food, even though they have to share it.

◄ A pair of Harris' hawks hunt a ground squirrel together.

▲ COLLARED LIZARD

For the collared lizard, escaping from predators can be difficult, because it lives in open desert areas where there is little or no cover to hide behind. To escape quickly, the lizard runs on its hind legs. This is called bipedal locomotion.

Deserts

DESERT BASIN

There are a number of animals and plants that make the very hot and arid desert basin their home. They all tread a thin line between survival and death, constantly competing for food and water. Not even the best-adapted species can survive in the hottest, driest places.

▼ COYOTE

Coyotes are dogs that live in a variety of different **habitats**. This is because they are **opportunistic feeders**. Coyotes are both scavengers and hunters that can easily adapt to a changing food supply. They communicate with each other by howling, especially at night.

▲ SAGUARO FLOWER

In the desert, flowering plants, such as the saguaro cactus, cannot always rely on insects to pollinate them. The saguaro flower is large and colorful, with a sugary nectar. Long-nosed bats and hummingbirds are attracted to the flower. When they drink the nectar, pollen gets on their bodies. The animals then carry the pollen from one plant to another.

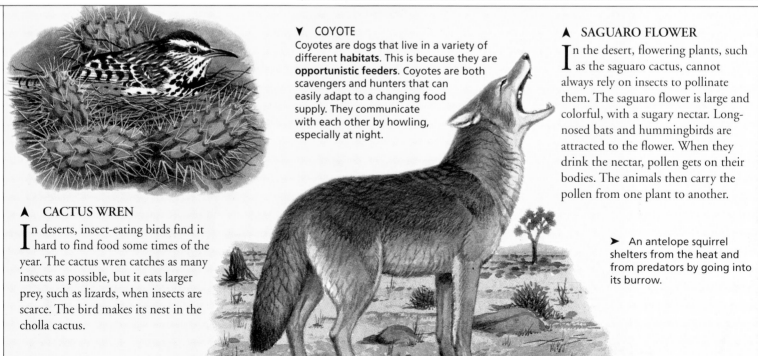

▲ CACTUS WREN

In deserts, insect-eating birds find it hard to find food some times of the year. The cactus wren catches as many insects as possible, but it eats larger prey, such as lizards, when insects are scarce. The bird makes its nest in the cholla cactus.

➤ An antelope squirrel shelters from the heat and from predators by going into its burrow.

◄ ELF OWL

Elf owls are named for their small size. They prey on **invertebrates** and small **vertebrates**. Their small size means they do not need to eat large amounts of food. Elf owls nest in small holes, such as the holes made in the stems of cacti by gila woodpeckers. The owls cannot make the nest holes themselves because of their small beaks.

▲ ASH-THROATED FLYCATCHER

Several species of flycatcher inhabit the desert. The ash-throated flycatcher often makes its home in nest holes abandoned by gila woodpeckers.

▼ KANGAROO RAT

The kangaroo rat is a rodent. It is not related to kangaroos, but gets its name from having large, kangaroo-like back legs that it uses to speedily hop away from danger.

GILA WOODPECKER ➤

In the desert there are few trees for woodpeckers to use for their nest holes. Instead, they use the stems of large cactus plants, such as the saguaro. The inside of the cactus is mostly water, but the woodpecker has a dry nest hole because the cactus produces **scar tissue** that forms a protective and waterproof shell. The gila woodpecker also feeds on insect larvae living in the cactus stems.

TARANTULA HAWK WASP ▼

There are several types of wasp around the world that prey on spiders. Tarantulas are very large spiders of the desert, but even they have to watch out for the tarantula hawk wasp. The wasp paralyzes the spider with its sting and then brings it to the burrow to feed to its **larvae**.

▼ CHUCKWALLA

The chuckwalla protects itself from predators by hiding under rocks. It has very loose skin, so it can inflate its lungs with air until it wedges itself inside rock crevices. The chuckwalla never strays very far from its rocky habitat, because it has no other defense against predators.

◄ ANTELOPE SQUIRREL

Antelope squirrels live in family groups in burrows beneath the desert surface. Like all squirrels, they do not eat meat, but feed on plants, and roots that they dig from the ground.

▼ The gila monster grips prey firmly in its mouth until its venom has worked.

▼ GILA MONSTER

The gila monster is a large lizard covered with shiny, pink and black bead-like scales. It is one of only two species of lizard with a poisonous bite. Unlike poisonous snakes, gila monsters do not have hollow fangs for injecting venom. Instead, **venom** flows along groves on their teeth when they bite into their prey. Gila monsters have a thick tail for storing fat, which allows them to go for months without eating.

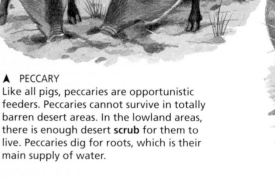

▲ PECCARY

Like all pigs, peccaries are opportunistic feeders. Peccaries cannot survive in totally barren desert areas. In the lowland areas, there is enough desert **scrub** for them to live. Peccaries dig for roots, which is their main supply of water.

Deserts

LOWLAND DESERT

Deserts get their name because they have supposedly been deserted by life. This is not true for the lowland part of the desert, despite its severe conditions. The lowland is populated by many plants, and animals, such as the burrowing desert tortoise, that are well-adapted to survive the dry heat. Life is still thinly scattered in most of this region, because water is scarce.

JOSHUA TREE ➤

The blooms of the Joshua tree grow in erect spikes so that pollinating animals can easily locate them. The Joshua tree is one of the few trees that grow in the desert. It got its name because the branches reminded people of the **biblical prophet** Joshua, his arms stretched out in blessing.

▲ ATTRACTIVE FLOWERS

Flowers need a lot of water. Desert plants need to produce flowers in order to attract pollinating animals. The colorful flowers shown here are purple mats (top), desert dandelions (left), and desert sand verbena (right).

AMERICAN KESTREL ➤

Sometimes called the American sparrowhawk, this brightly colored bird preys on songbirds, small **mammals** and reptiles, and insects. Kestrels have the ability to hover, or flutter in one spot.

◄ WHITE-THROATED WOODRAT

Otherwise known as packrats, white-throated woodrats are rodents that gather pieces of deadwood. They use the wood to build mounds around their nests. As well as hiding their nests from enemies, the wood protects the rats from the hot sun and cold nights by acting as a layer of insulation. After several years of gathering the wood, the nests are as large as three feet (1 m) across.

➤ The white-throated woodrat leaves its nest at night to eat cacti.

▲ PYRRHULOXIA

The pyrrhuloxia is a small perching bird that is sometimes called the gray cardinal, because it is closely related to the bright red cardinal. The pyrrhuloxia has a very strong bill which it uses to crack open the tough seeds of desert plants.

▼ GAMBEL'S QUAIL

The deserts of the south-western United States sometimes feature steep-sided **gullies** eroded by flash floods. These gullies are called arroyos, and are home to animals such as the Gambel's quail. The quails produce a large number of eggs after a flood so that the chicks can feed on the new plant growth, insects, and seeds that follow. By producing as many **offspring** as possible, the birds make up for the high number of birds eaten by predators during the other parts of the year.

CUSHION CACTUS ➤

One of the many colorful cacti of the desert, the cushion cactus is a small plant with bright flowers. The flowers are pink, red, lavender, or yellow-green, and are surrounded by small bundles of spines.

TURKEY VULTURE ▲

This vulture gets its name because it looks similar to a wild turkey. The turkey vulture is a scavenger, which eats just about anything, including rotting carcasses. Also known as the turkey buzzard, it feeds and roosts in flocks. Turkey vultures **migrate** to South America in winter.

➤ The desert tortoise leaves its burrow to feed in the early morning or at dusk.

▼ DESERT TORTOISE

The desert tortoise eats the fleshy parts of plants, but can go without food for long periods of time. It digs underground burrows to shelter from the heat. The desert tortoise can live for decades.

HORNED LIZARDS ▼

These members of the iguana **family** are also called horned toads because their body has a flat, toad-like shape. Horned lizards make their eyes bleed when they are threatened. This deters predators by fooling them into thinking the lizard is diseased. For most predators, **instinct** tells them it is too risky to feed on flesh that may cause them illness.

▼ Horned lizards can make their eyes bleed when threatened.

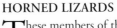

◄ PRONGHORN

The pronghorn looks like a deer, but it is the only member of a family that lies between antelopes and cattle. The pronghorn has forked horns, and a white rump that it uses to warn others of danger. Pronghorns used to be common mammals across North America, but its population has dropped in many areas as humans have increasingly **encroached** on its habitat. Its population survives mostly in deserts now.

◄ TRAPDOOR SPIDERS

The trapdoor spider digs a burrow and covers it with a hinged lid made of mud and silk. The spider listens for crawling insects, then bursts through the trapdoor to attack them. The hidden burrow also protects the spider and its young from predators.

▼ KIT FOX

Nocturnal animals in the desert avoid the daytime heat. This means that predators will be active at the same time as many prey animals. The kit fox, also called the swift fox, hunts rodents at night, and because of its large ears, has good hearing.

Deserts

DESERT VALLEY

The desert valley provides a good example of how desert life changes from the heat of the day to the coolness of the night. Pronghorns and jackrabbits are examples of animals that are diurnal, or active during the day. Nocturnal animals, such as the burrowing owl and the kit fox, are active at night. Deserts lack cloud cover at night. Clouds keep the air warm at night by acting as a layer of insulation.

ROADRUNNER ▼

Roadrunners mainly feed on insects and small vertebrates. The roadrunner spends much of its time on the ground and is a poor flier, with small wings and weak flight muscles. The roadrunner gets its name from its habit of racing along roads in front of moving vehicles before darting off to safety. It can reach speeds of fifteen miles per hour (25 km/h).

MONARCH BUTTERFLY ▲

Monarchs are famous for their annual north-south migrations over North America. They travel north-east to Canada in spring to lay eggs on milkweed plants. The new butterflies then fly south-west to Mexico in the autumn to **hibernate**.

DESERT LILIES ▼►

Lilies are a large family of flowers that also includes tulips and hyacinths. Desert lilies grow from bulbs that lie **dormant** under the ground. The strong scent of their flowers attracts pollinating animals. The flowers shown here are the desert mariposa tulip (below left), sand lily (below right), and lonely lily (top).

◀ Costa's hummingbird usually drinks from red flowers. The bird soars up and down as it moves between one flower cluster and another.

COSTA'S ➤ HUMMINGBIRD

Hummingbirds build tiny, delicate nests. They are small birds that hover as they feed. This allows them to collect nectar and pollen from flowers that are too weak to perch on. Both nectar and pollen provide the bird with water which is essential in the desert.

▲ PATCH-NOSE SNAKE

Snakes are well adapted to desert habitats. Their shape allows them to hide in places that other animals cannot fit into. Their shape also enables the snakes to catch prey in burrows or between rocks, where other predators cannot reach.

▲ The patch-nose snake has a blunt nose shield that helps it burrow in the sand.

OCOTILLO ➤

Flowering plants in deserts need to attract pollinating animals as quickly as possible, before their blooms dry up from the heat of the sun. The ocotillo attracts animals by its bright red flowers, which are highly visible across the desert. The plant is also covered in thorns to deter **herbivores** from eating it.

▼ BURROWING OWL

Just as the elf owl has adapted to desert life by nesting inside cactus stems, the burrowing owl nests inside burrows in the ground. In places where few cacti grow, the ground offers the best place to live. Burrows provide shelter from the heat and from predators.

▲ FRINGE-TOED LIZARD

Loose, dry sand can be difficult to move across, and as a result, life threatening for an animal that needs to catch its prey or escape from predators. The fringe-toed lizard has fringes of skin on its toes that provide a better grip by spreading its weight as it runs. Without the fringes, loose sand would move, and the lizard would slip backwards a little with each step.

◀ An owl perching at the entrance to its burrow.

WHITE-WINGED ➤ DOVE

White-winged doves are common in mesquite brush. They nest low down in cactus plants and eat the fruit of cacti such as the prickly pear.

▼ BLACK-TAILED JACKRABBIT

Jackrabbits are hares, not rabbits. The black-tailed jackrabbit is one of four species of hares that live in American deserts. The hares have very large ears, which perform two important functions. They help detect predators, and they act as **radiators**, so the animals can lose heat from their blood to cool themselves down.

◄ RINGTAIL

The ringtail, also called a cacomistle or ring-tailed cat, is a relative of the raccoon. Ringtails live in a variety of habitats, because they feed on almost anything. The ringtail is a nocturnal species that hides in its rocky den during the heat of the day. It emerges at night to find whatever food is available, such as small mammals, reptiles, insects, and berries. Ringtails are excellent climbers. They climb on both rocks and trees, and come down head first at high speed.

▲ DESERT SWALLOWTAIL

Swallowtail butterflies have large wings for gliding over long distances in search of plants to feed their caterpillars. The butterflies have extensions on their hind wings that look like the tails of swallows. The desert swallowtail is black or yellow.

▼ SCORPIONS

Scorpions are arachnids, a group of animals that also includes spiders. Scorpions are found in most warm parts of the world. Although scorpions are known for their poisonous stings, they use them only as a last resort when defending themselves. The venom needs to be saved for killing prey. Scorpions perform a courtship dance before **mating**.

Deserts

UPLAND DESERT

At higher altitudes the desert is less arid. More precipitation falls at higher altitudes and this allows more plant life to grow. Many more animals can survive because of this increase in plant life. These less arid parts of the desert are called semi-desert. Semi-desert regions have many different habitats that are dependent on the availability of water.

LEAST CHIPMUNK ►

The least chipmunk is the smallest chipmunk in North America. A member of the squirrel family that lives in sagebrushes, the chipmunk is an expert tree-climber. It spends most of its time in late summer and autumn collecting seeds, nuts, fungi, and berries. The chipmunk gathers the food into its cheek pouches and then takes it underground to store it. The chipmunk wakes a few times over the winter to feed, instead of relying on its extra body fat to survive, as true hibernators do.

▲ TESSELLATED RACERUNNER

Many lizards shed their tails when attacked by predators. While the detached tail wriggles as a **decoy,** the lizard makes its getaway in the confusion.

▲ MESQUITE AND SAGEBRUSH

Mesquite and sagebrush grow where there is moisture under the ground. Both mesquite (left) and sagebrush (right) are leafy plants that survive in the desert because their roots reach down very deep to the **water table**.

► The strong front claws of the badger make it a very quick digger.

▼ MULE DEER

As the desert gives way to mountainous terrain, more leafy shrubs, herbs, grasses, and the occasional pool of water appear in the landscape. The water helps plants grow and this allows the mule deer to find enough food to survive. Larger predators such as the puma can also survive because they eat the mule deer. The mule deer gets its name from its large, furry ears, which resemble those of a mule.

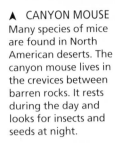

▲ CANYON MOUSE

Many species of mice are found in North American deserts. The canyon mouse lives in the crevices between barren rocks. It rests during the day and looks for insects and seeds at night.

➤ The mule deer has large ears, like a mule.

PRAIRIE FALCON ➤

Prairie falcons live in grasslands as well as semi-desert areas. They hunt for other birds and small mammals by flying high and lunging down for the kill when prey is located. Prairie falcons nest on rocky ledges to keep their young away from predators. Cliffs also provide the birds with a good view of the ground below, so they do not always have to fly around in search of food.

◀ SPOTTED SKUNK

Skunks are boldly marked in black and white as a warning to predators. If threatened, skunks raise their tail and puff themselves up to look fierce. If that fails to deter the predator, they squirt a foul liquid from **glands** in their rear end into the face of the attacker. This leaves the attacker stunned while the skunk heads to a safer spot.

▲ The skunk stands on its forefeet as a final warning to predators.

POOR-WILL ➤

Poor-wills hunt flying insects like swifts do, but at night. They have large, gaping mouths to catch moths and beetles, which are detected by a combination of senses. The poor-will is one of the few birds that hibernate.

◀ AMERICAN BADGER

Badgers are mammals that live in a variety of habitats, including semi-desert areas. Badgers are tough animals with thick, coarse fur, so they can prey on snakes without being fatally bitten. They also have some **resistance** to snake venom.

DIAMONDBACK RATTLESNAKE ▲

Rattlesnakes, or rattlers, belong to a group of poisonous snakes known as pit vipers. Rattlesnakes have **sensory pits** near their eyes that enable them to detect warm-blooded prey at night. The rattle is made from a series of hollow scales and is used to warn off predators.

Deserts

KEY TO FOLD-OUT

Use these key numbers if you want to identify the animals and plants on the Deserts fold-out. Most of them are featured on pages 12-19, and they are listed here in bold type. Plants and animals that are not featured are also keyed and listed here, with a brief description.

11 **Kangaroo Rat**
12 Desert Checkerspot
    This butterfly is a common sight after wet winters as it feeds on desert flowers.
13 Barrel Cactus
    One of more than 30 species of barrel cactus with large spherical or cylindrical bodies, this one starts out round and develops into an unbranched column with yellow flowers near the top.
14 **Cactus Wren**
15 **Collared Lizard**
16 **Coyote**
17 Organ-Pipe Cactus
    A big cactus, this species grows in a group like an organ.

Least Chipmunk (70)

1 **Harris' Hawk**
2 **Ash-Throated Flycatcher**
3 Western Coral Snake
    The red and yellow touching bands on this western coral snake means it is poisonous
4 **Antelope Squirrel, Yuma**
5 **Chuckwalla**
6 **Tarantula Hawk Wasp**
7 **Gila Woodpecker**
8 **Saguaro**
9 **Elf Owl**
10 Teddy Bear Cholla
    This species of cholla cactus branches out from a woody stem and bears yellow or pale green flowers in spring.

18 **Turkey Vulture**
19 Western Tiger Swallowtail
    These butterflies gather in large numbers at puddles or streams in western canyons.
20 **Gila Monster**
21 **Desert Sand Verbena**
22 **Desert Tortoise**
23 Cactus Mouse
    This mouse belongs to the family of white-footed mice, which are active at night and feed on seeds.
24 Prickly Pear
    This cactus has fleshy, leaf-like lobes that expand in size to hold moisture when it rains. It has protective spines instead of leaves.

25 Short-Tailed Black Swallowtail
These butterflies are powerful flyers. They drink damp earth, which also provides them with other nutrients they need.

26 Leopard Lizard
Leopard lizards get their names because of their round, dark spots. This species is related to the collared lizard but has no collar.

27 **American Kestrel**

28 **Pyrrhuloxia**

29 **Peccary**

30 **Gambel's Quail**

31 **White-Throated Woodrat**

32 **Desert Dandelion**

33 **Horned Lizard**

42 Loggerhead Shrike
Shrikes often stick prey, such as mice, lizards, and small birds, onto thorns, before tearing it to pieces to eat.

43 Gridiron-Tailed Lizard
One of the speediest lizards, this species tries to avoid extremes of temperature.

44 **Ocotillo**

45 **Costa's Hummingbird**

46 Claret Cup Cactus
The flowers of this cactus bloom on top of its ribbed stems in early summer.

47 **Fringe-Toed Lizard**

48 **Patch-Nose Snake**

49 Western Fence Lizard
This spiny lizard has blue sides.

59 **Sagebrush**

60 **White-Winged Dove**

61 **Prairie Falcon**

62 Gray Fox
This fox is also known as the tree fox.

63 **Ringtail**

64 **Tesselated Racerunner**

65 **Badger**

66 Sara Orangetip
This butterfly lives in a wide variety of habitats, including desert canyons.

67 **Scorpion**

68 **Poor-Will**

69 Western Racer
Western racers constrict, or strangle, their prey.

White-Winged Dove (60)

34 **Purple Mat**

35 **Cushion Cactus**

36 **Joshua Tree**

37 **Black-Tailed Jackrabbit**

38 Desert Lily
The strongly perfumed, white funnel-shaped flowers of the desert lily attract hummingbirds and other pollinating animals. Their bulbs taste like onions and were eaten by some Native North Americans.

39 **Kit Fox**

40 Ruddy Copper
Found in sagebrush and open, dry areas, this butterfly is a fast flier.

41 **Lonely Lily**

50 **Burrowing Owl**

51 **Trapdoor Spider**

52 **Monarch Butterfly**

53 Desert Hyacinth
Like the desert lily, this flower is also a member of the onion family and was once used as food.

54 **Desert Mariposa Tulip**

55 **Roadrunner**

56 **Sand Lily**

57 **Pronghorn**

58 American Century Plant
Also called the agave, this plant, grows as tall as 30 feet (9 m). It got its name by mistake because it was thought to bloom only once every 100 years.

70 **Least Chipmunk**

71 **Puma**

72 **Mesquite**

73 **Desert Swallowtail**

74 **Mule Deer**

75 Great Desert Poppy
A large white flower, this species grows in loose, rocky desert.

76 **Canyon Mouse**

77 **Diamondback Rattlesnake**

78 **Spotted Skunk**

79 Dagger Pod
When the pods of this plant dry, the entire flowering stem breaks off at the base and is carried away by the wind.

Mountains

The Rocky Mountains are home to a wealth of wildlife that changes up or down the slopes. Altitude, or height, influences the landscape and the animals that live there. The farther up a mountain, the more specialized the animals and plants are to the habitat. The Rocky Mountains are located in western North America, running north-south from Alaska to New Mexico. The wildlife featured in this section is found in the Middle Rockies, which includes national parks such as Yellowstone in Wyoming.

▶ MOUNTAIN PEAKS

Depending on their altitude, the **summits** of mountains may be constantly covered in snow, or snow-covered only in winter. All summits are barren, because they lack soil for plants to grow. The only life found at the very top of the mountain is the occasional bird, and lichens. Lichens grow on rocks, even under cold windswept conditions.

▶ ALPINE PLANTS

The term alpine applies to any plant that grows high up on mountains. Alpine plants grow low to the ground to avoid the chilling winds. They also flower and produce seeds very rapidly, because the summer season is so short. Many alpine plants are grown and sold to people for their rock gardens.

◀ SHELTER

Animals find shelter in safe places, such as tree trunks and underground in burrows. Where there are no trees, rocks and boulders on mountain slopes provide some shelter for animals such as pikas.

▶ TREELINE MEADOWS

Above the **treeline** there is just enough soil for grasses, herbs, and shrubs to grow into ground-hugging meadows. These meadows are colorful when the plants flower in spring. The flowers attract flying insects, which pollinate the flowers while they feed on nectar and pollen.

LICHENS

Lichens are **fungi** that contain algae. Algae convert the sun's energy into food for the lichen. Lichens can then grow with only small amounts of chemicals taken from bare rocks, air, rainwater, and occasional bird droppings.

▼ FLOWERS

Flowers contain the **reproductive organs** of plants. To produce seeds, the female organs, called carpels, need to be fertilized with pollen from the male organs, or stamens. The petals of the flower attract pollinating animals.

▲ MOUNTAIN FORESTS

Mountain forests are dominated by fir trees, also called pines or conifers. Fir trees are evergreens, which means they keep their leaves all year. Needle-shaped leaves are better at conserving moisture, which can be scarce on mountainsides in winter. Fir-tree sap contains a natural **antifreeze** called methanol.

▲ VEGETATION

Deciduous trees and shrubs grow farther down the mountain slopes. Unlike evergreens, deciduous trees lose their leaves each autumn and grow new ones every spring. Many herbs also die off above ground in the winter and grow again in the summer.

▲ MOUNTAIN MEADOWS

On the lower slopes of mountains, the forests turn into meadows that thrive on fertile soils made from the minerals of eroded rocks. The meadows are good pastures for grazing animals and are, in turn, good hunting for predators. The mountain rivers that run through the meadows are also teeming with life, including fish and **amphibians**.

MOUNTAIN PEAKS

The summits of mountains are barren, but life exists a little farther down on the lower peaks. This is because soil gets blown by the wind into crevices and cracks, enabling plants to take root on the slopes. These plants keep the soil in place and provide food for animals to eat.

▼ WHITE-THROATED SWIFT

Swifts are skillful and, as their name suggests, fast flyers. The white-throated swift is the fastest-flying North American bird. It flies as fast as 200 miles per hour (320 km/h). They fly fast to catch flying insects.

▼ RAVEN

By weight, the raven is the largest of the passerines, or perching birds. The raven is much larger than its close relative, the crow. The raven is a scavenger, but also hunts other birds, such as pigeons and grouse. Ravens build messy nests on cliff ledges, which they defend when the nests are threatened.

▶ Ravens often feed on carrion, or the flesh of dead animals.

▶ The cones of the lodgepole pine (top) and the bristlecone pine (bottom).

▼ PEREGRINE FALCON

The peregrine falcon flies high and then dives to the ground with its wings closed to pick up speed when it spots prey. The falcon strikes its prey from above with its outstretched talons, knocking the prey to the ground. Falcon prey includes swifts, swallows, martins, and especially pigeons (shown below). These birds all fly in the open, which makes them easy targets.

▼ APOLLO BUTTERFLIES

Many insects visit mountain habitats, but Apollo butterflies are the most common and attractive. The caterpillars of Apollo butterflies feed on a variety of low-growing alpine plants, such as stonecrops, violets, saxifrages, and bilberry. The butterflies are large, with wingspans up to three inches (75 mm) across. The pale scales on the wings fall off as the butterfly gets older, so that the wings become transparent except for the black and red spots. This works as a form of **camouflage**.

WHITE-TAILED PTARMIGAN ▶

Ptarmigans live on the ground among the low-growing plants and rocks on the mountain slopes. Their plumage changes from summer to winter. In winter, they are completely white, which provides camouflage against the snowy background.

▼ MOUNTAIN FLOWERS

Mountain flowers are low growing, so the mountainside appears to be carpeted with a mosaic of colors. Insects travel from one flower to the next. The flowers shown here are (top to bottom): purple saxifrage, Rocky Mountain rockmat, alpine forget-me-not, and alpine saxifrage.

▶ MOUNTAIN GOAT

Mountain goats are not true goats, but a group of animals called "goat-antelopes." They rarely fight, except to defend their territory. Their thick wool protects them from the cold mountain winds, and their feet are designed for rock climbing. Mountain goat hooves have hard, outer edges for standing on rocks and soft, inner pads for gripping flat surfaces.

PINE TREES ▶

Pine trees, also known as firs or conifers, produce seeds in woody fruits called cones. Some animals eat the seeds, dropping some as they feed. This ensures that new trees will grow.

▶ SNOW BUNTING

Buntings are small, seed-eating birds, very similar to finches and sparrows. The snow bunting is a ground-living bird with contrasting plumage that acts as camouflage in places where patches of snow last through the year. During the breeding season, these birds pair up and keep to themselves, but at other times they travel in flocks with finches and larks. Grouping together provides safety in numbers from predators.

▶ BIGHORN SHEEP

The male bighorn sheep with the largest horns is the leader of the herd. To compete, males charge one another and butt their horns together. The fittest male claims the herd of females for mating. Female bighorns have horns, too, but they are smaller than the males'. Bighorn sheep live on the mountain slopes in groups of fifteen to twenty animals.

▼ The golden eagle soars with wings curved upward, looking for prey. It can carry prey as heavy as itself back to the nest.

▶ GOLDEN EAGLE

The golden eagle is a bird of prey. It is a skilled flyer, with good eyesight. The golden eagle can kill mammals as large as young deer, which it rips open with its hooked bill. Young eagles are called eaglets. They are raised in a cliff-top nest called an eyrie.

◀ The feet of the bighorn sheep (right), are adapted for climbing over rocky terrain. The feet of the white-tailed ptarmigan (left), have feathery toes that act like snowshoes.

▼ GOPHER SNAKE
Gophers are ground squirrels. The gopher snake hunts gophers and other rodents by entering their burrows. The prey is killed by **constriction** and swallowed head first.

▼ Gopher snake preying on a mouse.

► The rock wren is common on cliff faces and rock-strewn slopes.

▼► BIRDS OF THE TREELINE

At the edge of forests, the food available to birds are tree seeds, fruits, and insects. Clark's nutcracker (below) eats seeds from fir cones, while the canyon wren (further below) feeds on insects and spiders.

▼ GRIZZLY BEAR

Grizzly bears, or grizzlies, are a mountain species of the brown bear. Grizzly bears defend their territory. Their name comes from their grizzled, or gray-streaked, appearance, due to the white hairs that grow in their coat. Grizzly bears are bigger than black bears and will attack animals as large as deer.

► Two grizzly bear cubs have a playful fight.

Mountains

TREELINE MEADOWS

Above the mountain treeline the habitat is controlled by the changing seasons. The spring and summer seasons are short but produce a good supply of food. Many animals migrate up and down the mountainside searching for food. Other animals remain in the same area, hibernating in winter to conserve energy.

The male Cassin's finch (far right) has a bright red **crown**.

► NORTH AMERICAN PIKA
Pikas look like rabbits, but they are more like rodents. Pikas live on the rock-strewn slopes of mountains. During late summer, pikas collect and store dried plants and leaves in crevices for food to eat during the winter.

▲ CASSIN'S FINCH

Finches are seed-eating birds, but they catch insects and spiders to feed their young. Cassin's finches build their nests on the branches of conifer trees and feed their chicks a **regurgitated** mash of soft-bodied invertebrates, especially caterpillars. In autumn, when insects are scarce, they eat seeds and berries.

► A yellow-bellied marmot watches for predators.

▲ YELLOW-BELLIED MARMOT

Marmots are sometimes called groundhogs. They are chubby, ground-living rodents of the squirrel family. Marmots make burrows and feed on a variety of vegetation, including roots, stems, and bulbs. Yellow-bellied marmots take turns keeping a lookout for predators. When threatened, a marmot lets out a call so the others can all scurry to safety.

RED FOX ▲

Foxes are small members of the dog family. They live underground in dens that protect them from predators and the weather. Red foxes are carnivores that are found in Europe, Asia, and North America. They eat most things, including birds, small mammals, carrion, and fruit.

◄ Black bears are excellent tree-climbers that eat berries and other fruits.

VARYING HARE ►

The varying hare got its name because its **pelt** changes color from summer to winter. The hare molts, or loses, its fur so that it is brown in summer and white in winter.

► MINK

Mink are **semiaquatic** members of the weasel family. They hunt for birds, small mammals, and amphibians, and fish along streams and rivers. The North American mink has escaped into the wild in Europe from fur farms and has sometimes pushed out the native species.

► FLOWERING PLANTS

The flowering plants of the treeline meadows include (from left to right): long-leafed phlox, mountain kittentails, fringed gentian, old man of the mountains, sky pilot, and alpine laurel.

► PUMA

Also called the panther, the cougar, and the mountain lion, the puma is a large cat. Pumas are found from Canada to Argentina, usually in remote, mountainous areas. The puma hunts by stalking and ambushing. It leaps from rocks onto its prey's back.

▲ NORTH AMERICAN DIPPER

The dipper is a small bird that hunts invertebrates in mountain streams and rivers. The force of fast moving water holds it down while it searches under stones for food.

► Puma cubs have a spotted coat.

► BLACK BEAR

Black bears are smaller than brown bears. Black bears climb trees in search of birds' nests and fruit. They are **omnivores** that also eat fish and small mammals. Although their fur is usually black, some black bears have brown fur.

PILEATED WOODPECKER ➤

Woodpeckers vary in size, and they each rely on slightly different econiches, or sub-habitats. The large pileated woodpecker (far right) hammers at the rotten wood of tree trunks to dig out grubs. Smaller woodpeckers, such as the downy (top right) and three-toed (below), peck at the tree branches.

▼ BOBCAT

The bobcat and lynx may look alike, but they are different species. The bobcat has a slighter build, shorter fur, a shorter tail, and looks like a large domestic cat, except for the ear tufts. It hunts mammals and birds, stalking them before pouncing.

▲ HEMLOCK AND JUNIPER CONES

Hemlocks (cones, above top), and juniper are two of the evergreen trees of the mountain forest. The juniper has small fleshy cones, often called berries. Hemlocks are tall, graceful trees with a drooping tip.

Mountains

MOUNTAIN FORESTS

Some North American mountain forests have not been destroyed by people. The terrain is often too steep for logging or building, except for some ski resorts or log cabins. These forests are home to many animals that have lost their habitats elsewhere. It is a harsh environment for animals to survive in, especially during the winter.

➤ RED CROSSBILL

The red crossbill is a finch with a bill especially made for removing the seeds from fir cones. The **mandibles** cross over at the tips so they can get the seeds. The red crossbill only lives in forests with fir trees, where cones are available all year. The female (shown right) is not red.

➤ NORTH AMERICAN FLYING SQUIRREL

North American flying squirrels live in the **canopy** of the forest. They glide between trees using the skin that stretches between their limbs. This flap folds away when not in use (as shown here).

STELLER'S JAY ➤

Jays are members of the crow family that live in woodland and scrubland habitats. They eat a wide variety of food, including the chicks and eggs of other birds. Of the species of jay found in mountain forests, Steller's jay (above right) is easily recognized by the crest of feathers on top of its head. Other species include the grey jay (right) and the pinyon jay (far right).

▼ The male wapiti protects his females.

◀ GREAT HORNED OWL
The great horned owl is a large owl that hunts bigger mammals, birds, and reptiles. It has tufts of feathers on top of its head that look like horns. The owl uses old nest holes of other birds of prey, such as crows and hawks, built in rocks or trees.

MOUNTAIN CHICKADEE ▶
Chickadees belong to the titmouse family of small birds that live in woodlands. There are seven species of chickadee in North America. The mountain species has a white strip around its eyes. It is common in high altitude coniferous forests, but spends the winter in lower altitudes.

MOUNTAIN BLUEBIRD ▶
Mountain bluebirds are small thrushes that nest in tree cavities or old woodpecker holes. They feed their young flying insects, caterpillars, and spiders. Of the three kinds of North American bluebirds, only the mountain bluebird has no chestnut coloring in its plumage.

WOLF ▶
The wolf, or timber wolf, is a hunter of larger herbivores in the mountain forest. The wolf is not very big, but hunts in organized packs. Wolves run down and surround prey so that it is unable to defend itself. Wolves were becoming rare in some mountain forests, but scientists are now moving in wolves from other areas to increase their population.

▶ A pack of wolves killing a white-tailed deer.

▲ WAPITI
Wapiti, or elk, is a giant race of the red deer. The male has a chestnut-colored coat and large branching antlers. During the **rutting** season, males group together on display grounds called leks. They lock antlers with one another to compete for control of the herd. The strongest males take control of the herds of females.

▶ AMERICAN MARTEN
Martens are tree-dwelling members of the weasel family. They are skillful climbers that prey on squirrels. Martens also eat the chicks and eggs of birds. American martens make their dens inside the trunks of dead trees.

RED SQUIRREL ▶
Red squirrels live in coniferous forests. They eat the seeds from fir cones, leaving behind a stripped, woody core. The rusty color of their fur works as camouflage, because the needles of conifers turn the same color when they die on the branches. The squirrels sit very still while they feed, so that predators do not spot them.

▶ The stripped cone, after the seeds have been eaten.

Mountains

MOUNTAIN MEADOWS

Mountain meadows have moist and fertile soil, which is ideal for plants to grow. Along with plants, a healthy number of invertebrates are found. The plants and invertebrates provide enough food for vertebrates, such as mammals, birds, reptiles, amphibians, and fish. The result is a habitat busy with life all year around, especially during the spring and summer seasons.

RACCOON ►

The raccoon is one of the most widespread mammals of North America. Raccoons can find something to eat in most habitats. In mountain meadows, raccoons eat frogs, fish, birds' eggs, fruit, nuts, and seeds. It makes its den in trees or hollow logs.

◄ COMMON WESTERN SKINK

Skinks are lizards adapted to burrowing in loose soil and **humus**. They have short legs, pointed snouts, and smooth scales. The common western skink feeds on insects and other invertebrates during the summer. The female encircles her eggs until they hatch.

▼ BROAD-TAILED HUMMINGBIRD

The broad-tailed hummingbird feeds on flowers in the forest. Eight species of hummingbird nest in the mountainous regions of North America. Hummingbirds feed on nectar, pollen, and small insects. They migrate seasonally, sometimes traveling thousands of miles. Hummingbirds hover while feeding, beating their wings rapidly to stay in the same place.

► MOUNTAIN BUTTERFLIES

Butterflies of mountain habitats only fly for two or three weeks. The rest of the season the butterflies are developing as larvae, or caterpillars. The larvae have a difficult time finding food because of unpredictable weather. The butterflies shown in flight (above) are common alpines, the one feeding (right) is a rockslide alpine.

◄ RED-TAILED HAWK

The red-tailed hawk hunts rodents, rabbits, and hares in the meadow. They spot their prey by flying over their territory, circling and soaring on rising **air currents**, or by using high perches to survey the ground. The birds choose isolated trees for their nests, where they raise one to four chicks, depending on the availability of food.

MOUNTAIN COTTONTAIL ►

The mountain cottontail gets its name because its tail looks like a tuft of cotton on a cotton plant. It uses its tail to signal danger to other rabbits.

SAW-WHET OWL ►

This small owl is named for its call, which sounds like a saw blade being whetted, or sharpened.

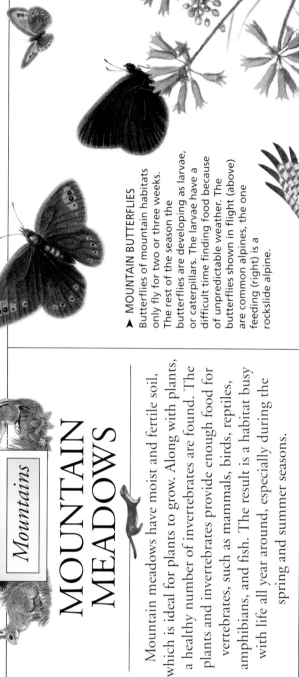

RED-BREASTED NUTHATCH ▶

Nuthatches search for insects by patrolling tree trunks from top to bottom. They also feed on the seeds of pine cones. The red-breasted nuthatch chooses a natural cavity or old woodpecker's hole to nest in, but it can also make its own nest hole in soft, rotten wood. When a nest hole entrance is too wide, the nuthatch lines it with mud.

◀▼ A sequence showing how a hummingbird flies. It beats its wings about 80 times a second.

▶ MOOSE
The moose is the largest species of deer. It lives in habitats containing wetland. Moose feed on semiaquatic plants while wallowing in water to avoid the biting flies.

◀ BLUE GROUSE
The blue grouse is a ground bird that nests at the edge of the mountain forest, within a short distance of the meadow. The blue grouse cock inflates its neck sacs (seen as a red and white patch) to make his **courtship** hooting louder. The female raises the chicks without the male.

◀ A broad-tailed hummingbird approaches a flower to feed.

▶ YELLOW-PINE CHIPMUNK

Chipmunks are squirrels that **forage** for food both on the ground and up in trees. They nest in burrows beneath tree roots or rock piles. The yellow-pine chipmunk eats seeds, nuts, and fruit to store as fat for winter, but it is not a true hibernator. The chipmunk wakes over the winter to eat food it has stored under the snow.

▶ MOUNTAIN MEADOW FLOWERS

The flowers that grow in mountain meadows are tall and strong. The flowers compete for soil space, sunlight, and moisture with a variety of grasses. This rich plant life means a variety of animals can live there. The hay from the meadows make a highly nutritious fodder, or feed, for livestock in nearby farming communities. The blooms shown below (from left to right) are: firecracker flower, mission bells, cascade lily, and wood lily.

◀ LONG-TAILED WEASEL
The long-tailed weasel is a predator of small rodents. Like all weasels, it has a slender body so that it can chase rodents inside their burrows. The weasel sometimes stands on its hind legs to catch birds.

MOUNTAINS

Mountains

KEY TO FOLD-OUT

Use these key numbers if you want to identify the animals and plants on the Mountains fold-out. Most of them are featured on pages 28-35, and they are listed here in bold type. Animals that are not featured are also keyed and listed here with a brief description.

1 Raven
2 White-Throated Swift
3 Peregrine Falcon
4 North American Bighorn
5 White-Tailed Ptarmigan
6 Golden Eagle
7 Townsend's Solitaire
  Related to thrushes, Townsend's solitaire winters lower down, where it feeds on juniper berries.
8 Snow Bunting
9 Bristlecone Pine
10 Clodius Parnassian Butterfly
11 Mountain Goat
12 Alpine Saxifrage
13 Rocky Mountain Rockmat
14 Lodgepole Pine
15 Alpine Forget-me-Not
16 Purple Saxifrage
17 Grizzly Bear

Mountain Goat (11)

Broad-Tailed Hummingbird (69)

48 Wolf
49 Purplish Copper Butterfly
   This is the most common western copper butterfly. Coppers are notable for their orange-red color.
50 Pileated Woodpecker
51 Great Horned Owl
52 Bobcat
53 Williamson's Sapsucker
   Birds of the woodpecker family, sapsuckers make small holes in the bark of trees to get the sap. They also eat insects and ants. Unlike other sapsuckers, the Williamson's sapsucker does little harm to the trees.
54 Juniper
55 Wapiti
56 White-Tailed Deer
   The underside of this deer's tail is white, and this shows as a warning signal when the tail is raised during flight from danger.
57 Red-Breasted Nuthatch
58 Raccoon
59 Moose
60 Silvery Blue Butterfly
   Blues are a large subfamily of butterflies. This slow-flying blue is found in a variety of habitats, especially the Rockies.
61 Saw-Whet Owl
62 Common Western Skink
63 Blue Grouse
64 Yellow-Pine Chipmunk

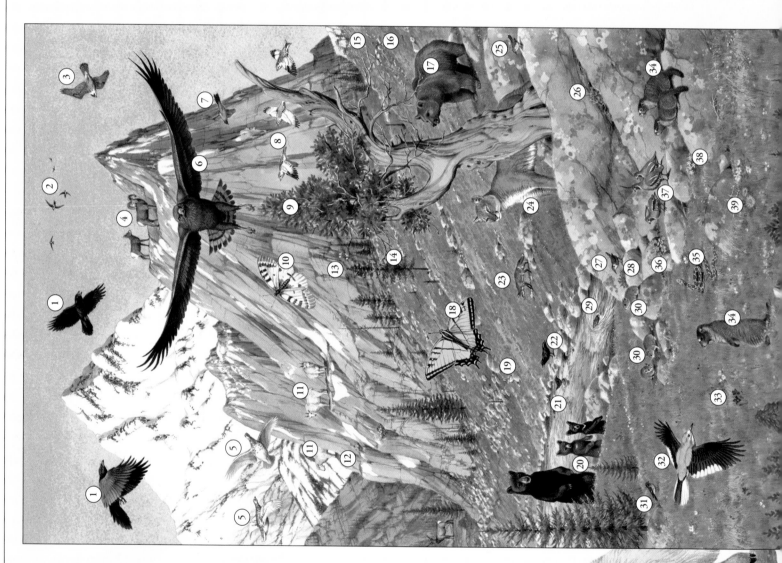

18 **Two-Tailed Tiger Swallowtail**
A familiar butterfly in backyards,
this swallowtail is also found in
mountain and desert canyons.

19 **Varying Hare**
20 **Black Bear**
21 **North American Dipper**
22 **American Crow**
The crow is common throughout
North America. It flaps its wings
steadily and has a straight-line flight.
The crow's feet are well-adapted for
walking. Crows eats a variety of
food, including seeds, fruit, nuts,
and small mammals and birds.

23 **Red Fox**
24 **Puma**
25 **Rock Wren**
26 **Alpine Laurel**
27 **Canyon Wren**
28 **Sky Pilot**
29 **Mink**
30 **North American Pika**
31 **Cassin's Finch**
32 **Clark's Nutcracker**
33 **Fringed gentian**
34 **Yellow-Bellied Marmot**
35 **Gopher Snake**
36 **Mountain Kittentails**
37 **Mountain Quail**
The largest quail, this species
measures up to eleven inches (29 c
m) and has long, straight head
plumes. They visit the mountain
slopes up to 10,000 feet (3,000 m)
in summer, but winter lower down.

38 **Long-Leafed Phlox**
39 **Old Man of the Mountains**
40 **Steller's Jay**
41 **North American Flying Squirrel**
42 **Mountain Chickadee**
43 **Red Crossbill**
44 **Red Squirrel**
45 **Hemlock**
46 **American Marten**
47 **Mountain Bluebird**

65 White Virgin's Bower
Also called the pepper vine, this
climbing plant was used by North
American natives as a cure for colds.

66 **Cascade Lily**
67 **Red-Tailed Hawk**
68 **Firecracker Flower**
69 **Broad-Tailed Hummingbird**
70 **Rocky Mountain Bee Plant**
This plant produces a lot of nectar,
and attracts many bees.

71 **Prairie Rattlesnake**
The prairie rattlesnake lives at high
altitudes as well as on the prairies.

72 **Mountain Cottontail**
73 **Rockslide Alpine Butterfly**
74 **Anise Swallowtail**
This butterfly is adaptable to many
habitats, from the sea to the
mountains.

75 Arrow Leaf Balsam Root
This yellow flower grows on open
hillsides. The native peoples once
used its root in medicines.

76 **Mission Bells**
77 **Long-Tailed Weasel**
78 **Common Alpine Butterfly**
79 **Alpine Lily**
This white flower, is found growing
in rock crevices up to high altitudes.

80 Alpine Buttercup
This flower is closely related to other
buttercups, such as clematis and
anemones.

81 Pinyon Mouse
The pinyon mouse makes its home
under rocks. This mouse is also a
good climber and gets juniper seeds
and pine nuts from the small pine
called the pinyon.

82 **Wood Lily**

Gopher Snake (35)

MOUNTAINS AND DESERTS

——— GLOSSARY ———

adapted Describes a plant or animal that has become well suited to its environment

air currents Bodies of air from one direction that are moving through still air

altitude Height above sea level

amphibians Animals that live in the water and breathe through gills at the larvae stage, then live on land and breathe in through lungs at the adult stage

antifreeze A substance added to water so the water will not freeze as quickly

arid A climate that is so dry that little plant life can survive

biblical prophet A teacher from a religious holy book, the Bible, who interprets, or explains the meaning of, the word of God

birds of prey Birds that hunt animals for food

burrow An animal's underground home

camouflage Coloring or shape matching the surroundings

canopy The upper branches and leaves of trees

carcasses The dead bodies of animals

class Living things are grouped by scientists in a system called taxonomy. The largest grouping is a kingdom. Animals and plants are further divided into a phylum. A class of plants and animals is a grouping within a phylum

commodity A useful thing

constriction The method that some snakes use to kill prey in which the snake tightens its body around the prey

courtship The behavior of animals before mating

crown The top part of a bird's head

decoy An object used to trick or lure an animal

dormant A plant or animal that is alive, but not developing or growing

encroach To intrude, or move in, on something else's territory

erode To gradually be worn or washed away by water, wind, or chemicals

evaporate To turn from a liquid or solid state into a gas

family A taxonomic division below order. A family is a group of related animals

flash floods Floods caused by sudden and heavy rainfall

forage To go looking for food

fungi Organisms, or living things, that are neither plants nor animals and that produce spores instead of seeds

gland An organ in the body that lets out liquid

gully A channel or small valley created by water erosion

habitats The natural places where plants and animals are found

herbivores Animals that eat plants

hibernate To become inactive during the winter

humid Air that contains a lot of moisture

humus A type of soil that is created from decayed, or rotting, plants and animals

instinct A natural reaction not controlled by thought

insulate A layer that prevents heat from escaping or entering

invertebrates Animals that lack a backbone

larvae Pre-adult stage of some invertebrates

mammals A group of warm-blooded animals whose bodies are covered with hair or fur. Female mammals make milk in their bodies to feed their young

mandibles The upper and lower parts of a beak or mouth

mating When two animals come together to breed, or produce offspring

migrate To move from one location to another in order to mate or find food and water

offspring An animal's young

omnivores Animals that eat both meat and plants

opportunistic feeders Animals that feed on a wide variety of animals and plants, depending on what is available

pelt The fur or hair of an animal

pollination To deliver pollen to a flower's carpel, or female part

predators Animals that hunt and kill others for food

prey An animal that is hunted by another animal

radiator Something that gives off heat energy

regurgitated Food that has been swallowed and then brought up again

reproductive organs Body parts of plants and animals, usually consisting of a male and a female part, whose role is to make offspring

resistance The ability to withstand something

rutting When male herd animals are sexually active

scar tissue A group of cells that combine to make a fibrous layer in a body or plant

scavengers Animals that hunt for dead animals or what remains of them, often stealing meat from other carnivores

scrub Habitat with dusty soil and scattered vegetation

semiaquatic Animals that spend part of the time on land and part of the time in the water, usually to hunt

sensory pits Holes in the skin made especially to detect something

species A group of similar living things whose offspring can reproduce

summits The highest points of mountains

treeline The dividing area in which trees can survive from where they cannot survive

venom A liquid poison produced by some animals

vertebrates Animals that possess a backbone

water table The level of the ground water beneath the surface

water vapor Water in a gaseous state

watercourses The bed along which a stream or river flows